WHY DO WE DO THAT?

101 Random, Interesting, and Wacky Things Humans Do -
The Facts, Science, & Trivia of Why We Do What We Do!

SCOTT MATTHEWS

Contents

The more that you read, the more things you will know. The more you learn, the more places you'll go.

- Dr. Seuss

Introduction

Have you ever found yourself wondering why humans do the things they do? Why, for instance, does the act of cutting an onion often lead to tears, or why do we feel compelled to kiss under a sprig of mistletoe during the holiday season? Humans engage in countless customs, rituals, and behaviors, both seemingly ordinary and utterly peculiar, and each one has a story to tell.

In *Why Do We Do That?* we embark on a remarkable journey to explore 101 random, interesting, and sometimes wacky things humans do. These rituals span the cultural and physical spectrum, offering a window into the fascinating diversity of human behavior.

We'll journey from the physical, where goosebumps rise and hair grays, to the cultural, where we celebrate birthdays with cake, exchange vows at weddings, and even mark days with fireworks.

Each chapter unravels a new facet of our humanity, exploring not only the "what" but also the "why" behind these actions.

You'll discover the science, history, and trivia that provide insight into our everyday and extraordinary behaviors.

As we journey through the pages, you'll gain a deeper appreciation for the quirks and curiosities that make us uniquely human. Together, we'll celebrate the intricate mosaic of human existence, one fascinating quirk at a time, and answer the age-old question, "Why do we do that?"

1. Crying when cutting onions

Television shows and movies often joke about people crying while cutting onions. Anybody who has cut an onion before knows that this is more than a joke as the onions can actually cause somebody to shed tears. This is because they contain a compound that irritates the human eye. Onions grow in the ground and absorb sulfur as they grow. Whenever you cut into an onion, the sulfur is released via a compound known as syn-Propanethial-S-oxide. Once this compound reaches your eyes, it causes certain glands in your eyes to produce tears in order to wash out the irritant. These glands are known as lacrimal glands. The tears produced by these glands help wash the sulfurous acid out of your eyes and prevent further irritation. Some people are more sensitive to the compound found in onions than others are. These individuals should consider wearing goggles, chilling or freezing onions before chopping them, or chopping the onions while they are underwater.

2. Kissing under the mistletoe

The tradition of kissing under the mistletoe is believed to have originated in pagan cultures in Europe. The plant was considered sacred by the Druids and was thought to have healing powers, as well as the ability to ward off evil spirits. In Norse mythology, the mistletoe was associated with the goddess of love, Frigg, who had a son named Baldr. According to legend, a mistletoe arrow killed Baldr, and his mother wept tears that turned into the mistletoe's white berries. Frigg then declared the plant a symbol of love and vowed to kiss anyone who passed under it. Over time, the tradition of kissing under the mistletoe became associated with Christmas. It is now a common holiday custom in many countries. The rules of the tradition vary, but generally, people who find themselves under the mistletoe are expected to exchange a kiss. Today, the mistletoe is often hung in doorways or other prominent places during the holiday season. It is considered good luck to kiss someone under the mistletoe.

3. Having allergies

Allergies are a common condition that can manifest in a variety of ways. For some people, they cause sneezing, watery eyes, and mild itching. For others, they can be more severe, causing problems breathing and issues with blood pressure. Allergies form when a person's body mistakes a harmless substance, such as the protein found in peanuts, for a dangerous invader such as a parasite. This causes the immune system to attack the allergen, causing the release of inflammatory cells and a variety of unpleasant symptoms. Allergies can often be treated by over-the-counter medication, but more severe cases may require allergen avoidance and usage of an epipen upon exposure. Sometimes, doctors will recommend special shots to people with allergies. These shots introduce small amounts of the allergen into a person's body, with the goal of increasing the amount the person can tolerate before their body reacts to the allergen.

4. Getting tattoos

People have been tattooing themselves since ancient times. In the past, many cultures such as ancient Egyptians and ancient Japanese people would get tattoos to identify themselves as part of their culture. Many other cultures also practice tattooing including that of indigenous American groups. Many of these tattoos were rooted in one's status within the community, religious beliefs, and personal record keeping. Tattoos have also been used to identify people, but these kinds of tattoos were not often received voluntarily. An example of this is the string of numbers often tattooed on Jewish prisoners during World War II. In modern times, people get tattoos primarily for decorative purposes. Often, they hold some meaning of significance to the person getting them. Some tattoos are meant to memorialize dead family members or celebrate events such as the birth of a child. However, many people get them simply because they like the way they look.

5. Getting goosebumps

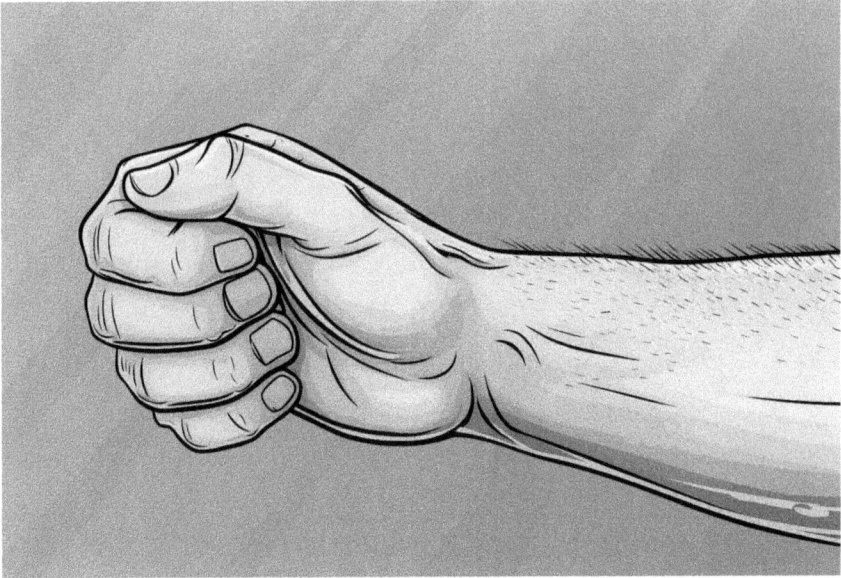

Have you ever wondered why you get goosebumps whenever you get cold or scared? Goosebumps are a remnant from a time when humans had thicker hair, dating back to a time before we were humans, when we still had fur. These tiny bumps appear when the small muscles in our hair follicles tense. This is an attempt to get our hair to raise up in a similar manner to how a cat's fur raises up whenever it is afraid. When this happens, it helps keep animals warm and helps them appear bigger. Thus, when we are cold, our bodies try to heat us up by puffing out our now nonexistent fur. When we are afraid, our bodies assume that we are facing a physical threat and attempt to make us seem bigger by fluffing up our invisible coats. While we no longer benefit from this ability, there has been no reason for our bodies to stop producing this effect. It is one of the odd things that are left over from the past when humans were very different than we are now.

6. Having leap years

During most years, February is a month composed of only twenty-eight days. However, every four years, February instead has twenty-nine days. This is called a leap year. Leap years happen because each year is based on one rotation around the sun. This rotation takes about 365 days plus an additional six hours. Instead of counting the six hours each year, we let the six hours build up until it reaches twenty-four hours total. Then, we add an extra day to that fourth year to count the twenty-four hours we collected. This allows our count to catch back up with the proper rotation of the Earth around the sun, without us having to deal with the inconvenience of putting a quarter of a day in our calendars each year. This extra day is known as Leap Day. People born on this day only celebrate their actual birthday every four years, thanks to leap years. How wacky is that?

7. Going bald

As men get older, it is common for them to begin to lose their hair. Some women also find themselves losing their hair, although usually it is not in the same pattern as males and is less noticeable in the early stages. This is usually caused by a specific hormone that shrinks the hair follicles on the head. The name of this hormone is dihydrotestosterone, or DHT. This hormone stimulates hair growth over the rest of the body while causing hair loss on the top of the head. Men naturally create more testosterone, which leads to a higher production of DHT. Women, on the other hand, produce estrogen, which often masks the effects of testosterone, delaying balding or preventing it altogether. The risk of going bald is closely related to genetics. Most individuals who experience balding have a father who went bald at a similar age. However, there are physical and emotional factors related to balding that are unrelated to genetics and DHT.

8. Smiling when happy

Smiling happens when humans raise the corners of their mouths. This is usually in response to positive emotion. For a long time, scientists believed this was a learned behavior. They assumed that babies learned how to smile from watching their parents and other adults smile. However, they soon realized this was not the case when they noticed blind infants learning to smile. Smiling is an innate behavior that is instinctual to humans. When humans feel happy, endorphins are produced, telling your brain it's time to smile. One interesting thing about smiling is that it is also possible to reverse this effect. By forcing yourself to smile or simply by using the muscles involved in smiling (such as your zygomaticus major muscle and orbicularis oculi muscle), you can cause your brain to release endorphins and make you happy. It's believed that this reflex developed as a way for humans to display positive emotions and promote social bonding without having to use language.

9. Jumping when startled

Most people have been frightened or surprised before, only to involuntarily shake or jump in response. This is known as the "startle response." This response begins in the brainstem. The body, sensing danger, readies itself to react. The brainstem causes it to react in a manner that allows one to quickly move in order to protect vital organs or flee the situation. This causes the muscles in the body to move rapidly in reflex, causing the person to "jump." If there is no valid threat, the response ends there. The person may make a noise as they jump, then may breathe heavily for a moment as the startle response disappears and they return to baseline. However, if there is a threat, the person will likely spring into action after, either getting into a defensive position or running away. Those who have experienced trauma in the past are often more easily startled due to their body being pre-primed to take action. This can cause some individuals to jump at unexpected situations more often than others.

10. Clinking glasses and saying cheers

The practice of clinking glasses and saying "cheers" is a common social practice used to show goodwill and friendship, often when toasting someone or something. It is a way of expressing good intentions and hoping the other person will have a good time. The practice of clinking glasses dates back to ancient Greek and Roman times, and the word "cheers" is derived from the Old French word "cher," which means "dear." Clinking glasses and saying "cheers" is a way to celebrate special occasions and show appreciation to others. Several theories exist about the origins of this habit. One theory is that the practice began to ward off evil spirits and demons, as the sound of glasses clinking and people cheering loudly was thought to scare them away. Another theory is that it developed to avoid poisoning, as mixing drinks and taking a sip was a way to show that the drinks were unharmed. A third theory states that it has roots in ancient customs of offering alcoholic beverages to the gods during celebrations or as a way of making a wish or prayer for health.

11. Blowing out candles on a birthday cake

Blowing out candles on a birthday cake is a tradition that has roots in ancient Greece, where round cakes with lit candles were placed on them to honor Artemis, the goddess of the moon. The cakes represented the moon, and the candles represented reflected moonlight. The smoke from the candles was believed to carry wishes and prayers to the gods. Using candles on a birthday cake also has roots in Germany, where a large candle was placed in the center of a cake to symbolize the light of life. Nowadays, birthday cakes are typically decorated with candles equal to the age of the person being celebrated. The person makes a wish before blowing out the candles. The blowing out of the candles is believed to fulfill a desire and end the celebration. It is often accompanied by the singing of "Happy Birthday." Superstitions surrounding blowing out birthday candles include the belief that the wish must be silent and that reusing birthday candles brings bad luck.

12. Tossing coins in fountains

The tradition of tossing coins into a fountain is a practice that has been around for centuries and is believed to have originated in early European cultures. Water is vital to sustaining human life, and in many regions, clean drinking water is only sometimes readily available. People in these places believed that areas with clean water were a gift from the gods, and wells and fountains were often considered shrines because of their association with clean water. It is thought that tossing coins into a fountain was developed to honor the gods or make a wish. In many cultures, fountains were believed to have magical or sacred properties, and it was thought that tossing a coin into a fountain would bring good luck or grant a wish. One theory about the origins of this tradition is that it dates back to ancient Rome, where fountains were often decorated with statues of gods or other mythical figures. It was believed that tossing a coin into a fountain and making a wish would please the gods and bring good luck. Another theory is that the practice originated in Europe, where fountains were often associated with good fortune and was thought to have the power to grant wishes.

13. Throwing rice at weddings

The tradition of throwing rice at weddings dates back to the Roman era and possibly even further. It is a way to wish the newlyweds good luck and prosperity, as rice symbolizes fertility and abundance in many cultures. In modern times, throwing rice at weddings has become a popular tradition in many parts of the world. It is often seen as a fun and lighthearted way to celebrate the newlyweds and wish them good luck and prosperity in their new life together. Recently, some couples have substituted rice with birdseed due to concerns that uncooked rice scattered on the ground could harm birds. However, there is no evidence to support this claim. Rice has also lost popularity due to the risk of someone slipping on it or getting a grain in the eye. In some countries, such as Italy, sugar-coated nuts or confectionaries are thrown, while wheat is used in France.

14. Trick or treat

Trick-or-treating is a Halloween tradition in which children and sometimes adults dress up in costumes and go from house to house in their neighborhood asking for treats, such as candy, with the phrase "trick or treat." The origins of trick-or-treating can be traced back to the ancient Celtic festival of Samhain, which celebrated the end of the harvest season and the beginning of the winter season. During Samhain, the Celts believed that the boundaries between the living and the dead became blurred, and they thought that the ghosts of the dead returned to Earth. The Celts would leave out food and drink offerings to appease these ghosts and prevent them from causing mischief. The modern version of trick-or-treating originated in the United States in the 1930s. However, similar traditions have been documented in other countries, including England and Canada.

15. Baby showers

Baby showers are a celebration of the expectant mother and the upcoming birth of her child. They typically involve the expectant mother receiving gifts and well wishes from friends and family, and the mother's close friends often organize them. The origins of baby showers are difficult to trace. Still, they are thought to have originated in ancient civilizations, where pregnant women were showered with gifts and well wishes to ensure a safe and healthy delivery. In the United States, baby showers as we know them today began to gain popularity in the early 20th century. In the past, it was more common for baby showers to be held after the baby's birth. Today, it's more common for them to be held in the last trimester of pregnancy. Baby showers are now a popular celebration in many countries around the world. They are a way for friends and family to show their support for the expectant mother and to help her prepare for the arrival of her new baby.

16. Prom

Prom, short for promenade, is a formal dance or gathering of high school students. It is typically held near the end of the academic year and is a significant event for many teenagers. The origins of prom can be traced back to the late 19th century when it was common for colleges and universities to host formal balls. These events, called "proms," were held to celebrate the end of the academic year and allow students to socialize and dance. In the early 20th century, proms began to be held at high schools, and they became a major social event for high school students. They typically involve the selection of a prom king and queen, and they often include other activities such as dinner, dancing, and the crowning of the prom court. Today, prom is a popular event at high schools worldwide and is often seen as a rite of passage for many teenagers.

17. Milk and cookies for Santa

The tradition of leaving milk and cookies out for Santa on Christmas Eve is a longstanding one that many families worldwide practice. The origins of this tradition are still being determined. It is thought to have originated in the United States in the 1930s and 1940s. The custom of leaving out milk and cookies for Santa is believed to have started as a way for children to express their excitement and anticipation for Christmas, and to show their appreciation for all of the gifts that Santa brings.

18. Measuring in inches / using Fahrenheit

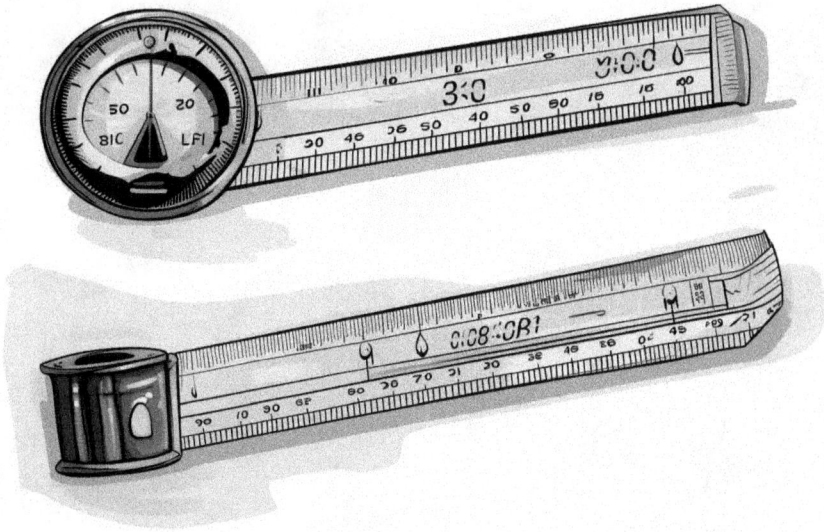

On one hand, an inch is a unit of length equal to 1/12 of a foot (2.54 centimeters). It is commonly used as a standard unit of measurement in the United States, Canada, and several other countries. The inch is derived from the Latin "uncia," which means "one-twelth," and was initially based on the width of a human thumb. In ancient civilizations such as the Roman Empire, the inch was used as a standard unit of measurement, and it has continued to be used in this way throughout the centuries. On the other hand, the Fahrenheit scale is based on the temperature at which water freezes and boils. In this scale, the freezing point of water is thirty-two degrees Fahrenheit, and the boiling point of water is 212 degrees Fahrenheit. The Fahrenheit scale is named after the German physicist Daniel Gabriel Fahrenheit, who proposed it in 1724. In contrast, the Celsius scale, or the centigrade scale, is based on the temperature at which water freezes and boils at sea level. In the Celsius scale, the freezing point of water is zero degrees, and the boiling point of water is 100 degrees.

19. Lightning bonfires

Bonfires have a long history and have been used for various purposes throughout the centuries. The word "bonfire" comes from the Old English "bonefire," which means "fire of bones," and it originally referred to a large fire that was used to burn bones. Bonfires have been used for many purposes throughout history, including disposing of waste, cooking food, and providing warmth and light. They have also been used for ceremonial and cultural purposes. In many ancient cultures, they were used as part of religious rituals and ceremonies, often associated with spiritual and magical practices. In more recent times, bonfires have been used to celebrate holidays and special events, such as Independence Day in the United States and Guy Fawkes Day in the United Kingdom.

20. Bursting fireworks

People burst fireworks for various reasons, including celebration, entertainment, and commemoration. Fireworks are often used to mark special occasions such as holidays, weddings, and sporting events. They also celebrate national and cultural events such as New Year's Eve, Independence Day, and Chinese New Year. Fireworks have been used for centuries as entertainment, with displays becoming more elaborate and sophisticated over time. People of all ages enjoy them, and they can create a sense of excitement and wonder. In addition to celebration and entertainment, fireworks can be used for commemoration. For example, they are often used to honor the memory of loved ones who have passed away or to commemorate significant historical events. Overall, bursting fireworks has become a popular way for humans to express joy, happiness, and a sense of unity and togetherness.

Did You Know?

- Humans are the only species known to engage in recreational activities for fun.
- The average person spends about six years of their life dreaming.
- Your taste buds are replaced every ten to fourteen days.
- Human beings have unique fingerprints, tongue prints, and footprints.
- We shed about 600,000 particles of skin every hour.
- Humans are one of the few animals capable of crying emotional tears.
- Laughter is a universal human behavior, transcending cultural boundaries.

21. Housewarming parties

Housewarming parties are a traditional way of welcoming friends, family, and acquaintances to a new home. The origins of this practice can be traced back to ancient times when people would light a fire in a new home to symbolize warmth, light, and protection. In modern times, housewarming parties allow new homeowners to share their excitement about their new home with loved ones, show off their new space, and receive gifts to help them settle in. It's also a way for friends and family to congratulate the homeowners and help them celebrate this new chapter. Housewarming parties can take many forms, from casual gatherings to formal affairs. Some people choose to have a potluck or barbecue, while others may hire a caterer or host a dinner party. Regardless of the style, a housewarming party is a way for new homeowners to connect with their community and create new memories in their new homes.

22. Pinky swear

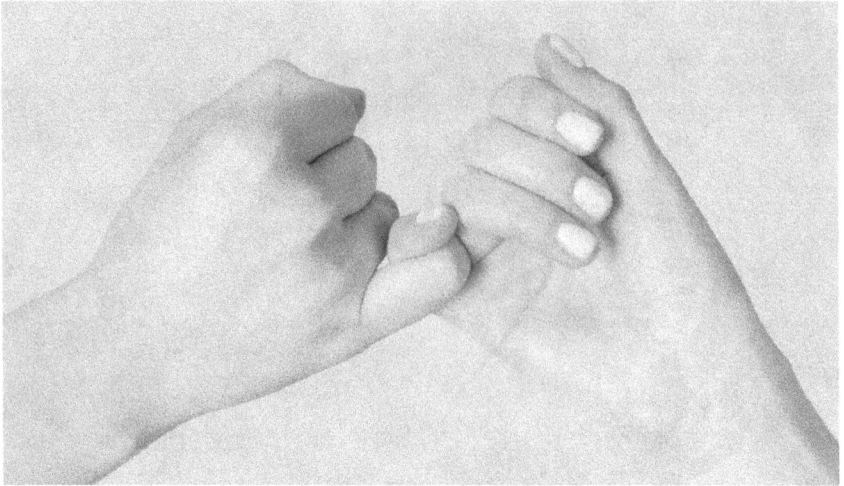

Pinky swearing, also known as "pinky promise," is a gesture of trust and commitment often used by children and young adults. The act involves linking pinky fingers with someone else and making a promise or vow. The origins of pinky swearing are partially unclear. It is believed to have started in Japan in the 17th century. According to some accounts, it was a way for samurai warriors to seal their promises by interlocking their little fingers. In Western cultures, pinky swearing has become a common way for children to make promises to each other. Linking pinkies is seen as a sign of sincerity and trust, and breaking a pinky promise is considered a serious breach of trust. Pinky swearing is often used to seal promises about important things to children, such as keeping a secret, sharing a toy, or being friends forever. It can also be a way for adults to make lighthearted promises, such as a pledge to meet up for coffee or to complete a task by a certain deadline. Ultimately, pinky swearing is a way for people to show their commitment to one another and to reinforce the importance of keeping one's word.

23. Getting yellow teeth

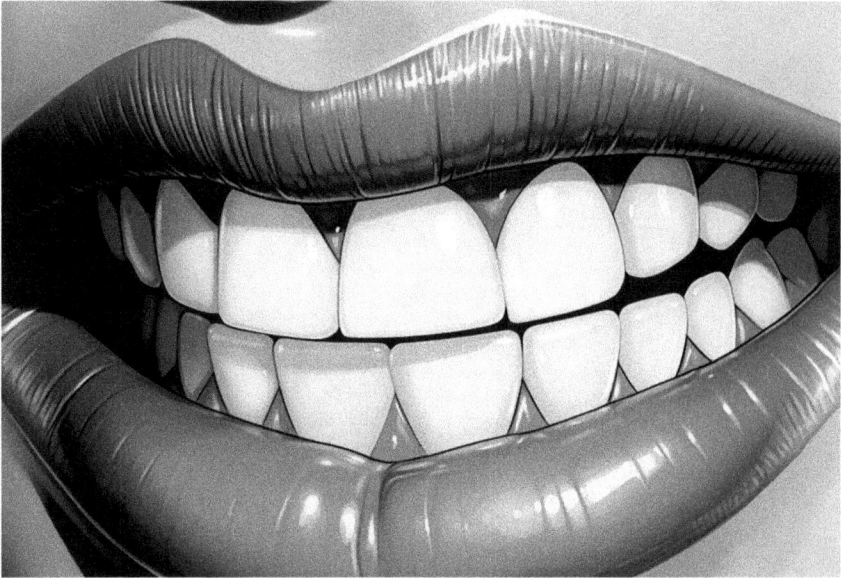

With time, many people notice a change in the color of their teeth, often turning from a bright white to various shades of yellow. This discoloration is primarily due to the dentin, a naturally yellow-hued tissue that lies beneath the enamel, becoming more visible as the outer hard enamel wears thin over the years. Enamel thinning can be caused by dietary choices such as consuming coffee, tea, wine, and foods with strong colorants, as well as lifestyle habits like smoking, which introduces tar and nicotine to the teeth, leading to stains. Additionally, the enamel is eroded by acidic foods and drinks, which roughen its surface, making it easier for pigments to latch on. The process is gradual but can be accelerated by poor dental hygiene, as plaque build-up can also cause a yellow appearance. It's also interesting to note that the color of one's teeth is partially determined by genetics, as the natural thickness and natural whiteness of enamel are traits that can be inherited from one's parents.

24. Election on Tuesdays

The tradition of holding US federal elections on Tuesdays dates back to the early 19th century. The decision to hold elections on a Tuesday was made for several reasons, including:

Farmers: In the early 19th century, most Americans were farmers. Tuesday was chosen as the election day because it allowed farmers to travel to the county seat, vote, and return home in time for market day, which was typically held on Wednesdays.

Religion: Sunday was not considered a good day to hold elections because it was a day of rest for many religious communities. In addition, Monday was not considered ideal because it would require people to travel on Sunday, which was unacceptable for many religious groups.

Travel: In the 19th century, long distances were difficult and time-consuming. Tuesday was chosen as the election day because it gave people enough time to travel to the polls without interfering with other important activities or commitments.

Since then, the tradition of holding federal elections on Tuesdays has been maintained, even though many of the original reasons for choosing that day are no longer relevant. Today, some people argue that holding elections on Tuesdays may discourage voter turnout, particularly among working people who may find it difficult to take time off to vote. However, changing the election day would require a significant overhaul of the US election system and is unlikely to happen in the near future.

25. High five

A high five is a celebratory gesture that involves slapping palms with another person. It is typically used to express excitement or congratulations, which has become a common form of nonverbal communication in many parts of the world. The origins of the high five are not entirely clear, but it is believed to have started in the world of sports. Some sources credit the University of Louisville basketball team in the 1970s with popularizing the gesture, while others point to a Los Angeles Dodgers baseball player named Glenn Burke, who was known for giving his teammates high fives. Regardless of its origins, the high five quickly became a popular form of celebration among athletes and fans alike. The gesture is often used to celebrate a victory or a good play. It has become common for people to show their support and enthusiasm for one another. Today, the high five is used in many settings, from sports arenas to offices and schools. It's a simple and effective way to show appreciation and build camaraderie.

26. Easter eggs

The origins of Easter eggs can be traced back to ancient pagan traditions, which celebrated the arrival of spring and the renewal of life. Eggs were seen as a symbol of fertility and rebirth, often used in rituals and ceremonies to bring good luck and prosperity. When Christianity became the dominant religion in Europe, many pagan traditions associated with the spring festival were absorbed into the Christian celebration of Easter. The egg, which had long been a symbol of new life and rebirth, came to be associated with the resurrection of Jesus Christ and the promise of eternal life. In many cultures, the tradition of decorating eggs for Easter began as a way to celebrate the arrival of spring and the renewal of the natural world. For example, the ancient Greeks and Romans would dye eggs bright colors and exchange them as gifts during the spring festival of Ostara. The practice was later adopted by Christians, who would decorate eggs in the colors of the church, such as red, to represent the blood of Christ.

27. Celebrating St. Patrick's Day

St. Patrick's Day is a holiday that originated in Ireland and is celebrated worldwide on March 17th. The holiday is named after St. Patrick, the patron saint of Ireland, who brought Christianity to the Irish people in the 5th century. St. Patrick's Day has been celebrated in Ireland for over a thousand years. In the 17th century, the holiday began to take on its modern form. The first St. Patrick's Day parade was held in New York City in 1762. The holiday has since become a popular cultural celebration for people of Irish descent worldwide. St. Patrick's Day is a national holiday in Ireland, and parades, festivals, and other celebrations typically mark it. The color green, associated with Ireland, is a common theme of this day, and many people wear green clothing or accessories on holiday. Today, St. Patrick's Day is celebrated in many different countries and it has become a symbol of Irish culture and heritage worldwide. While the holiday has its roots in religious tradition, it is now largely a secular celebration of Irish history and culture.

28. Decorating a Christmas tree

The tradition of decorating a Christmas tree dates back to ancient pagan cultures in Europe, which celebrated the winter solstice with evergreen trees and branches as a symbol of life and rebirth. The practice of bringing trees indoors and decorating them with ornaments and candles was later adopted by Christians as part of their Christmas celebrations. The modern Christmas tree tradition is often traced back to Germany in the 16th century when trees were decorated with candles and other ornaments as part of the Christmas celebration. The custom eventually spread throughout Europe and was brought to North America by German immigrants in the 18th and 19th centuries. Today, the Christmas tree is a popular symbol of the holiday season in many parts of the world. It is often the centerpiece of holiday decorations in homes, churches, and public spaces. The tree is typically adorned with lights, tinsel, ornaments, and other decorations. It's seen as a symbol of hope, joy, and renewal during the dark days of winter.

29. Having funerals

While the concept and practices of funerals differ throughout various locations and cultures, recognizing and celebrating those who have recently died is a practice that most human cultures share. While the practice is generally accepted as normal, many people who think deeply about it wonder exactly how it got started and why it's so popular. The answer lies in religious beliefs. Throughout history, many religions had beliefs about how one had to behave in life and had to be treated after death in order to make it to the afterlife. Archaeological records show that ancient humans and even Neanderthals had certain rituals they performed once somebody had died. The modern version of this process began with the ancient Egyptians, when they began embalming and mummifying their dead, as they believed that the bodies would be used in the afterlife. In general, scholars classify funerals as having five components: symbols, gathering of community, rituals, culture, and transition of the body. Together, these components form an elaborate religious rite that allows individuals to begin the mourning of their loved ones.

30. Honeymoon

Honeymoons have an interesting history rooted in practices that are very foreign to modern humans. The original honeymoon was not a vacation. Instead, it was a period of time where a bride was kept away from her family after being captured by somebody who wished to wed her. During this time, men chose their wives by stealing them instead of winning them over. During the honeymoon, the couple would hide from individuals who would potentially want to stop them from being wed. Our more modern version of a honeymoon began in the 19th century. Couples would take something called a bridal tour. During the tour, they would visit relatives and friends who were unable to attend the wedding. Eventually, this turned into a simple vacation taken by a newlywed couple for the purpose of enjoying their marriage. Commercial airlines made the possibilities for this vacation a lot more exotic and now couples will sometimes travel across the world in celebration of their love.

31. Thumbs up

The origins of using the thumbs up and thumbs down signs are somewhat disputed. Some experts who study gorillas have noticed that many animals with opposable thumbs will also do the signal. This indicates that the signal may have developed naturally from a celebration of having opposable thumbs. Others argue that the animals seen doing the signals likely witnessed them being done by humans and are merely imitating them. The first historical record of the usage of the thumb signal is during gladiator battles. Ancient Romans would have the crowds give a thumbs up or thumbs down to indicate how they felt about a particular contestant specifically after defeat. It's believed that giving a thumbs up meant that the crowd was voting for the gladiator to be killed. Later, the signal was used by medieval archers to show that they were ready for battle. It wasn't until World War One that the signal became synonymous with saying that something was good or enjoyable. Afterward, it slowly gained traction in the Western world.

32. Signing with our signature

Signatures are used to show the identity of somebody signing a document. This began with the ancient Sumerians. However, instead of writing their name in a special style, they simply stamped a personal seal identifying themselves. Eventually, this led to the Sumerians using written names as their signatures. This was used to show the identity of somebody, usually the author of the written document. In modern times, signatures can also be used to show that documents are authentic. They are sometimes legally binding and are used to show that somebody agrees to all terms of a contract, is willing to follow that contract, and accepts the consequences that come if they break it. Forging signatures, or writing somebody else's signature on a document can be considered fraud in certain circumstances and open up somebody to legal punishment and lawsuits. There are some concerns with the rise of technology leading to the usage of e-signatures which can sometimes be as simple as somebody typing a name into a document.

33. Saying "love" in tennis

In tennis, a score of zero is often referred to as "love." This term has baffled many individuals watching the sport. Some claim that the history behind it lies in the shape of the number zero. The French noticed that the number looked like an egg, specifically that of a goose or duck. They began calling it such, with the French word for an egg being *l'œuf*. English speakers, mishearing the word, began calling it "love" instead. However, etymologists claim there is little proof for this theory. Instead, some say it likely comes from the idea of "playing for the love of the game." Players who score no points but continue to play are likely not playing to win. Thus, it is believed they are playing for "love." This relates to the term amateur, as "amare" means to love in Latin. This indicates that an amateur is somebody who plays for the love of the game, giving some credibility to the theory of "love" in tennis.

34. Gender reveal parties

We have all seen videos online of blue balloons bursting out of a box or a pink confetti coming out of a cannon while family members scream and jump in excitement. Gender reveals are parties that people have in order to inform their friends and family of the gender of their unborn child. Sometimes, the lucky parents will keep it a secret from even themselves, having a trusted friend or family member stuff the confetti into the piñata or having a local baker bake either pink or blue inside of the cake. This practice originated in the late 2000s. Individuals wanted to be able to inform their loved ones of their babies' gender in a fun, creative manner. Sometimes, this is done to let family and friends know what type of items to buy for the little one. Other times, it is an opportunity to present the name chosen for the child. In other instances, it's just a chance to celebrate with loved ones.

35. Muscle cramps

Muscle cramps are sudden, involuntary contractions that usually strike the leg muscles, causing intense pain. These spasms may be attributed to several factors, with muscle fatigue and nerve dysfunction at the forefront. When muscles are overused or in a static position for too long, the nervous system might trigger excessive contractions. Electrolyte imbalances also play a significant role. Key minerals like sodium, potassium, calcium, and magnesium are crucial for muscle function, and their depletion, often through heavy sweating during exercise or heat, can prompt cramps. Dehydration exacerbates this imbalance, leading to more frequent and intense cramps. Genetic predisposition and aging affect how susceptible individuals are to muscle cramps. As we age, muscles naturally lose mass and tire more easily, increasing cramp occurrences.

36. Saying "bless you" when somebody sneezes

There are a few different theories as to why people say "bless you" when somebody sneezes. Scholars say that these three theories are the most likely to be true. First, it's believed that in medieval times, people thought that your soul left your body when you sneezed. Saying "bless you" was either supposed to prevent a demon from inhabiting one's body before their soul could get back in it or it would force their soul to return to their body. Another theory behind this also begins in the medieval time, when people would say "bless you" if somebody sneezed as it could be a sign that somebody had the pneumonic plague. This is a version of the Black Death that killed a large amount of people during this time. The final theory states that people used to believe your heart would stop when you sneeze. Saying "bless you" was showing your hope that their heart would continue beating afterward and it would not be the end of their lives. In modern times, it's simply a culturally acceptable way to respond to somebody sneezing and it shows manners.

37. Feeling cold when we have fever

The idea of feeling cold while your body is at a higher temperature that it's supposed to be seems counterintuitive. Fevers often happen when individuals are fighting off an illness and are an attempt by the body to kill the germs via heat. Whenever this happens, your brain notices the germs and sets your internal body temperature to be higher than the normal body temperature (98.6 degrees Fahrenheit/thirty-seven degrees Celsius) a person has. The rest of your body will begin feeling cold and shivering as it tries to generate the heat necessary to reach the new threshold your brain has set. If your body is successful, the newly generated heat will prevent germs from multiplying while your immune system kills them off. Some fevers, especially low-grade fevers that are only slightly different than your average body temperature, may not produce as many chills or cold feelings as higher fevers. If the chills become too much, plenty of medications are available that prevent fever and return your temperature to baseline.

38. Having dandruff

Many television shows joke about people having dandruff, which is a condition that causes white, itchy flakes to form on your scalp. However, very few know the cause of the condition. Most people assume that dandruff is simply caused by dry skin, but this assumption is incorrect. In reality, there are several causes of the condition; one of them is seborrheic dermatitis, which causes an oily build-up and irritated skin. Other factors that can also lead to dandruff are eczema, ringworm, and contact dermatitis. Finally, one of the most common causes of dandruff is a yeast-like fungus called *malassezia*. In people with overactive immune systems, the body can attack this fungus and cause increased irritation of the scalp. Dandruff is usually treated with special, medicated shampoos. However, if an underlying condition, such as ringworm, is causing it, it may also need specialized treatment. Otherwise, the dandruff will likely return.

39. Using Dalmatians as firehouse mascots

Today, many firehouses and fire departments use Dalmatians as their mascot. While this is primarily symbolic in current times, in the past this athletic breed of dog played a more active role in fire rescue. Before they were modern fire engines, there were carts that had to be pulled by horses with the necessary rescue supplies mounted on top. In order to have a clear, safe path, dogs were made to run ahead of the horses in order to create the necessary path. Dalmatians work well with horses, unlike many other breeds who become easily startled by the large animals or tend to get in their way. Thus, this breed was commonly the first choice when fire departments were choosing dogs to join the team. Now, the Dalmatian acts primarily as a mascot, with many departments having logos involving the breed. Sometimes, modern departments will even keep a live Dalmatian as a firehouse pet. However, they do not actually work for the department as they did in the past.

40. Choking on our own spit

Everybody has had experiences where they find themselves choking on their own saliva. Many people wonder why this happens to humans considering it doesn't appear to happen to any other animal species. The part of the respiratory system that allows for breathing and the part of the digestive system that allows for swallowing are located right next to each other in the human body. Humans have a special body part that is supposed to prevent food from going into the respiratory tract and is supposed to allow it to instead enter the digestive tract. This body part is called the epiglottis and it relies on humans correctly swallowing and breathing at appropriate times. Failure to breathe or swallow at the proper time can lead to one inhaling food or swallowing air. When one inhales food, they choke. Sometimes, when one is swallowing their saliva, something similar happens and it causes them to choke on their own spit.

Did You Know?

- The human brain generates about 70,000 thoughts on an average day.
- Human DNA is 99.9% identical across all individuals.
- The human heart pumps approximately 2,000 gallons (7,570 liters) of blood daily.
- Humans are the only species that can blush.
- The brain can process information as fast as 394 feet (120 meters) per second.
- Humans are the only animals known to display empathy.
- Humans have the ability to taste five primary flavors: sweet, salty, sour, bitter, and umami.

41. Getting heartburn

Heartburn is caused by the regurgitation of food and stomach acid into the esophagus, which is the tube that connects the mouth to the stomach. The primary cause of acid reflux is due to an improperly working band of tissue at the bottom of the esophagus. This band of tissue is known as the lower esophageal sphincter and its job is to prevent stomach acid in food from going up your esophagus after it has made its way to your stomach. This sphincter is supposed to only relax when one is attempting to swallow food or water. Certain conditions may cause the sphincter to relax at inappropriate times which leads to reflux. There are many reasons this can happen including producing too much stomach acid, various gastrointestinal disorders, and high-fat, acidic meals. Everybody gets heartburn sometimes, but if it happens too often it can be a sign of gastroesophageal reflux disease (GERD). Heartburn is commonly treated with antacids and proton-pump inhibitors. Lifestyle changes, such as eating smaller meals and avoiding soda, can also help.

42. Cooking our food

There are multiple reasons why humans cook their food even when other animals do not. First, it makes a lot of food safer to eat. Bacteria and viruses, such as E. coli, are commonly found in uncooked meats. Cooking meat before eating it helps remove these harmful pathogens, making food safe to eat. If one does not cook their food, they risk developing food poisoning. In addition, cooking makes digestion easier. A lot of the food is partially broken down when cooked, making it easier to digest and giving it more calories than it would have if it were left raw. This allows us to get more energy from the food we eat. In addition, cooking food helps break down many of the nutrients necessary for our bodies to function, making it easier for our bodies to absorb these nutrients. Finally, cooking food adds flavor to the dish. A lot of raw foods lack taste and are unpleasant to eat due to texture. Cooking these foods enhances their taste and significantly eases consumption.

43. Mowing our lawns

Recently, many people have stopped mowing their lawns in order to create a better environment for pollinators and wildlife. Many have been asking why humans began mowing their lawns in the first place. Individuals began mowing the lawn as a way to ensure the visibility of their property. When grass was freshly cut, it provided a clear view of the entire property, allowing people to spot others and animals from a distance. It's believed that this practice began in England. During this time, it was not necessary for one to mow their own lawn with a lawnmower. Instead, sheep and cattle were allowed to graze which kept the grass low to the ground and generally of the same height. After years of this grazing, trimmed lawns became the expected landscaping. Thus, people have maintained their lawns through artificial means ever since. To some degree, this is still for visibility purposes. It's easy to see if there are any snakes or other dangerous wildlife in your walking path if the grass is cut short. However, overall it is mainly for aesthetic purposes.

44. Wearing socks

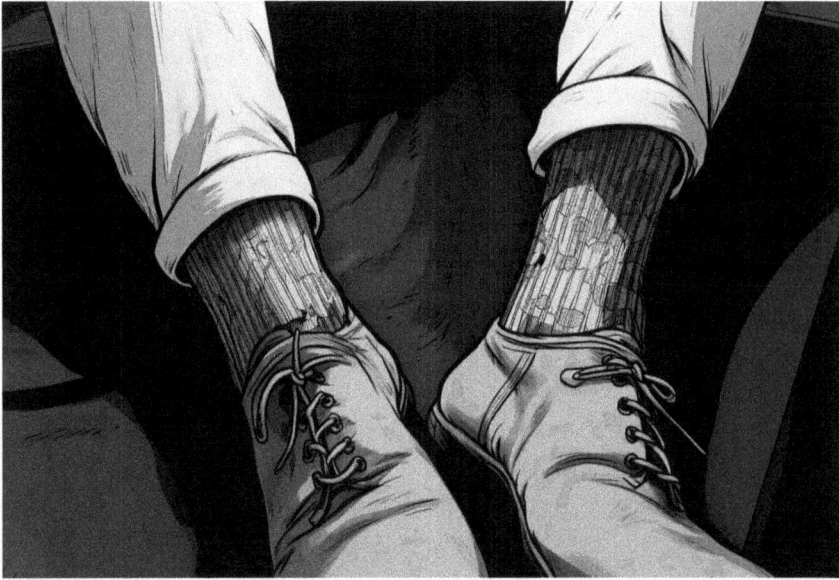

Humans wear socks for various reasons, with one of the primary purposes being to keep our feet warm. Frostbite is most common on the extremities such as the toes. Wearing socks can help prevent frostbite, and in less severe conditions, it prevents the uncomfortable feeling of cold feet. However, the cold is not the only thing that socks protect us from. They also protect our feet from moisture. By absorbing moisture, socks lessen the likelihood that we will develop fungus-related illnesses such as athlete's foot. In addition, they also prevent our feet from rubbing on the inside of our shoes and causing blisters. Plus, socks provide a barrier between your feet in the outside world, keeping any unpleasant smells away from the noses of those around you. Some socks are made to perform special tasks. Compression socks, for example, are designed to improve blood flow in the legs, benefiting athletes, individuals with jobs involving prolonged standing, and those with circulation issues.

45. Cutting our hair

Currently, humans primarily cut their hair for aesthetic purposes. People choose their hairstyles based on personal preferences and how they wish to look. However, this is not likely the reason that people began cutting their hair. The purpose of cutting one's hair originated in convenience and safety. Early humans began this practice to prevent it from being used against them in battle and to avoid interference with daily tasks. Long hair could easily be grabbed during fights or get caught in moving parts of various objects. Cutting long hair would ensure that these events did not happen. In addition, having long hair makes it more difficult to regulate one's body temperature in warm climates. Early humans also likely cut their hair in order to keep cool during warm summer months. Now, people primarily cut their hair to improve their appearance and maintain its health, including the removal of old or damaged strands.

46. Celebrating April 1st

April Fool's Day is a day filled with wacky fun and plenty of pranks. Kids everywhere love playing jokes on their friends and family. However, very few people know how this tradition originated. April Fools' Day began in 1582 when France transitioned from the Julian calendar to the Gregorian calendar. When following the Julian calendar, the beginning of the year began on the spring equinox, which was April 1st. However, the Gregorian calendar began on January 1st instead. Those following the Gregorian calendar began to make fun of those who were still following the Julian calendar. They mocked those who celebrated the start of the year in April, dubbing them "April fools" and playing pranks to ridicule them. Eventually, the tradition started making its way throughout Europe and eventually the rest of the world. Now, many countries celebrate April 1st as a day of pranks and fun.

47. Knocking on wood

Every day, people make comments and then state "knock on wood" or literally knock on wood afterward. The origin of this practice, however, is relatively unknown to most and dates back to ancient times. In the ancient world, when most people were pagan, they commonly believed that spirits inhabited inanimate objects, including trees. Almost all pagan religions included some belief in tree spirits. Thus, when people wanted to have good luck or were worried about having bad luck, they would knock on wood in an attempt to get the attention of the spirit within the wood. They believed that by doing this, the spirit would either bless them or protect them from bad luck. In the past, this was almost always done directly on a tree. Now, however, individuals will knock on anything made of wood. Sometimes, when wood cannot be found, people will just state "knock on wood" instead of actually doing the action.

48. Yawning

Yawning is something that humans do whenever they are tired. However, have you ever wondered exactly how yawning is supposed to help the situation? There are many theories as to why we yawn. The first and simplest theory is that the sudden action is meant to keep us awake and alert. Those who believe this theory state that yawning acts as an internal alarm system that prevents you from falling asleep. Opponents of this theory, however, state that this is not true as yawning does not really make you feel more awake. Recently, some scientists have developed a theory that yawning helps us get more oxygen to our brains. This is supposed to make us less tired. This also means that sometimes people may yawn when they aren't tired but are low on oxygen. Other scientists share a similar theory, suggesting it serves to cool down our brains. This also is supposed to help us feel more awake. Regardless of the theory, scientists agree on one thing about yawning: it is contagious.

49. Blinking

Humans blink for multiple reasons, with the first being to clear foreign material from the eye. Dust, pollen, and other irritants commonly get into the eye as we go throughout our daily lives. Blinking helps clear these irritants out before they can do damage to our eyes. In addition, blinking helps us lubricate our eyes. In order for our eyes to function properly, they must be moist at all times. This moisture helps light bounce off of our eyes, allowing for clear vision. If our eyes become dry, our vision suffers. When we blink, something called a tear film is released. This is a special coating made of mucus, oil, and water that is meant to keep the eye smooth. This coating also acts as a transporter, helping oxygen and special enzymes reach the eye. Oxygen sustains the eye and its proper function, while enzymes help combat potential eye-damaging bacteria. Ultimately, blinking is vital to eye health.

50. Sneezing

Sneezing is an uncontrollable reflex that humans have developed over time, occurring when the nasal passages become irritated. In an attempt to deal with this irritation, the body forces the nose to exhale air rapidly, resulting in a sneeze. This serves as the body's defense to prevent harmful invaders from reaching deeper into the respiratory tract. Sneezing is supposed to prevent one from inhaling viruses, bacteria, fungi, allergens, and other foreign bodies. The process begins with the mucous membranes in the nose registering that there is a foreign body touching the nasal passages. After, the trigeminal nerve is activated, which then activates the medulla oblongata (a part of the brain). This part of the brain activates the nervous system and tells it to increase tear and mucus production. The vocal cords close and pressure builds in the chest from a rapid inhale of air. This air is rapidly expelled through the throat and nose, creating a sneeze.

51. Passing gas

Passing gas is a gross but expected part of life. When we eat, we tend to swallow air. In addition, some of the foods we eat produce gasses when we digest them. These two factors lead to us developing pockets of gas or air that become trapped in our digestive system. This air cannot be absorbed, forcing us to pass the air out through our digestive system one way or another. When the air pocket is closer to the beginning of our digestive system and travels upward, it leads to burping. Often, we can feel the air building up in our upper stomach and esophagus before it makes its way out of our mouth. When the air is closer to the exit of our digestive system and begins to travel downward, it usually results in flatulence. This leads to a feeling of pressure in the large intestine and colon. When the air is expelled, it may make a noise we commonly call a "fart."

52. Getting grey hair

A majority of people are born with one of the following hair colors: black, brunette, blonde, or red. As we age, our hair may slowly begin to turn gray. While dying our hair can be a temporary remedy, it does not solve the issue. Some elderly individuals even start developing white hair after it has fully turned gray. Why does this happen? As we age, the cells in our hair lose their ability to produce melanin, a pigment that gives our hair its color. As the cells of your hair reproduce, the stem cells that create pigment slowly lose the ability to regenerate as you age. This leads to your hair beginning to gray as these cells die off and less melanin is produced. Most people start off with one or two gray hairs and slowly begin graying more and more as they get older. The older one gets, the less melanin they produce. If a person gets old enough, they may produce so little melanin that their hair turns white instead of gray.

53. Getting wrinkles

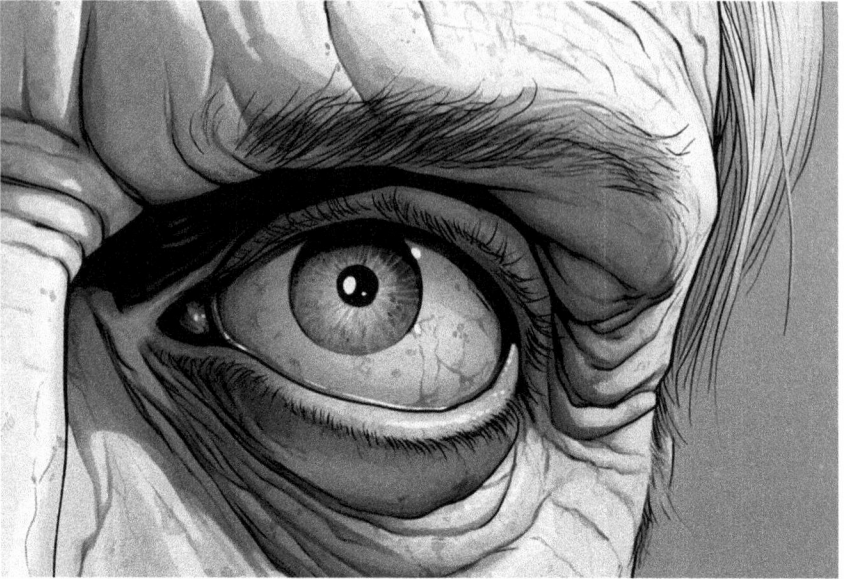

As we age, our skin naturally becomes less elastic, leading to the development of wrinkles. This is related to something called collagen, which is found in the middle layer of skin known as the dermis. As we age, our bodies produce less collagen, leading to our skin not retaining its original shape as much as it used to when we were younger. In addition, fat stored in the deeper layers of the skin is also altered by age and sometimes contributes to the development of wrinkles outside of the lack of collagen being produced. While developing wrinkles is natural, certain behaviors can exacerbate their appearance. Prolonged exposure to ultraviolet light in youth can lead to more noticeable wrinkles in old age. Likewise, smoking and tobacco use during youth can worsen wrinkles later in life by impacting collagen production. However, genetic factors play a significant role in determining the extent of wrinkle development, with daily habits having a lesser influence.

54. Hiccup

Hiccups are a common but annoying reflex that our bodies experience involuntarily. They often occur in a series and may persist for an extended period of time. For a very long time, scientists were unsure of why humans hiccup. Ultimately, it has been determined that the main reason we hiccup is because something is irritating our diaphragm muscle. The diaphragm is a muscle in the stomach that helps hold our internal organs in place and helps separate the chest from the stomach area. It also plays a vital role in the process of breathing. Whenever this muscle is bothered, it spasms in an attempt to get rid of the irritation. Internal factors, such as having air in your stomach, can lead to your diaphragm spasming. External factors, such as something touching the area outside of where your diaphragm is located, can occasionally also cause spasms. When the diaphragm is irritated, the nerves located in this area force the muscle to contract and aggressively expel air from your respiratory system, leading to a hiccup.

55. Sweating

Everyone has had the experience of sweating on a hot summer day. As you sweat, you find your hair and your skin growing moist. Perhaps you wondered what benefit this has. Sweating is a process that the body uses to cool itself. When your body feels that it's beginning to overheat, it informs a part of your brain called the "hypothalamus." This region of your brain forces your sweat glands to release sweat, which makes the surface of your skin moist. As this moisture evaporates, it cools your skin by using heat as energy, lowering your body temperature. However, this process also uses up the water in your body, as sweat primarily consists of water. Excessive sweating without replenishing lost fluids can lead to dehydration.

56. Getting headaches

Humans get headaches for a variety of reasons. The most common type of headache, referred to as a tension headache, usually results from overworked muscles in the neck, upper back, or head. Another common type of headache, called a sinus headache, is caused when your sinuses are clogged with mucus due to allergies or illness. This results in increased pressure against the nerve endings in your head, leading you to feel pain around your sinus cavities. Migraine headaches, which manifest as severe pain on one or both sides of the head, have no known cause. Scientists believe they may be produced by blood vessels in the brain narrowing unexpectedly. People who get migraines often have triggers that cause the headaches to appear. Some common migraine triggers are stress, caffeine, and lack of sleep. One type of headache, called cluster headache, is believed to be related to the release of histamine and its impact on the trigeminal (facial) nerve. This headache causes severe pain and is said to be even more painful than a migraine.

57. Blushing

Most people experience a moment or two in their life where they are embarrassed and find themselves blushing. Blushing can be triggered by any strong emotion, but it's typically associated with emotions such as anger, embarrassment, sadness, or fear. Blushing occurs when the small blood vessels in the face, known as capillaries, suddenly widen, allowing for increased blood flow. This happens when the nervous system is activated due to strong emotions or perceived threats. The brain tells the blood vessels in the body to dilate, leading to an increase in blood flow. The face has significantly more capillaries than other parts of the body, resulting in a noticeable reddening effect that occurs exclusively in this specific area. The cheeks, in particular, tend to redden more than other parts of the face. Ironically, humans often attempt to emulate this bodily function via the usage of makeup. This could be because humans sometimes blush due to romantic interest, making it appear attractive to other humans.

58. Wearing makeup

Modern humans wear makeup in order to display themselves in a manner that matches their personal senses of style or aesthetic. However, this was not always what makeup was used for and it is not the only way that it is used currently. Early Egyptians often wore makeup in an attempt to protect their faces from the heat of the sun. Some of the makeup worn in this culture also had antibacterial properties and helped prevent illness. Other cultures began adopting makeup primarily for cosmetic purposes, but some also used it to help protect their skin from the sun. Makeup has also been used in theater as it helps absorb some of the lighting so that the actors are not blinded or washed out by the stage lights. Often, simple makeup is used to hide blemishes, bruises, and scars that may make a person feel insecure. Overall, makeup has had a few different uses over the course of history.

59. Need to drink water

Humans need to drink water for a variety of reasons. First, water is used by the body to produce mucus and spit. The mucus is vital and protects our body from foreign invaders, while spit is an important factor that aids in digestion. Second, water is used to make blood, which is how the body transports oxygen. Third, water cushions and lubricates joints in our body, making movement possible. It also cushions the spine and brain, keeping them safe from harm. Water also helps us regulate our body temperature via sweat. In addition, it keeps the kidneys running smoothly and helps prevent constipation. It is also needed to dissolve and absorb nutrients, as well as to thin blood to make it the proper consistency to smoothly be pumped through the circulatory system. These are only the most basic ways water helps our bodies function.

60. Getting amnesia

Amnesia, or the inability to recall or create memories, can be caused by both physical and psychological problems. Strokes, which result from a lack of blood flow to the brain and can cause brain injury, can lead to amnesia. Brain inflammation, a lack of oxygen to the brain, alcohol misuse, brain tumors, seizures, and dementia can all cause amnesia as well. This is due to the way they often damage the hippocampus, which is the part of the brain that deals with memories. Individuals who damage this region of their brain may have issues recalling information or remembering new information. Psychological trauma can also lead to amnesia due to the brain not being able to handle memories of frightening events. This can result in people temporarily forgetting the traumatic event, omitting key details of the traumatic experience, having gaps in their memory surrounding the traumatic event, or experiencing a rare type of amnesia known as a "dissociative fugue" state.

Did You Know?

- The human eye can distinguish between 2.3 to 7.5 million different colors.
- On average, humans spend about twenty-five years of their life asleep.
- Humans are natural swimmers; infants can instinctively hold their breath underwater.
- The human skeleton is composed of 206 bones.
- Every year, humans produce enough saliva to fill two swimming pools.
- The strongest muscle in the human body is the masseter (jaw) muscle.
- The average person will spend approximately six months of their life waiting for red lights to turn green.

61. Sleeping

While scientists aren't quite sure why we sleep, they do have some plausible theories. One theory is that sleep is a state that we go in in order to conserve energy for the daytime. This theory states that nighttime is relatively dangerous in comparison to daytime. Ancient humans were unable to safely hunt, work, and play when the sun was down. In order to allow for the conservation of energy so that humans could do all of these activities during the day, we entered into a sleep state at night. Another theory is that sleep is necessary for the body to heal and in order for the brain to cleanse itself of toxins. The latest theory is similar; scientists believe that during sleep the pathways that connect our waking experiences to our memories strengthen, and that the brain's energy source replenishes itself. This is why a lack of sleep causes us to feel exhausted and struggle with memory. Ultimately, these are all still just theories, but sleep science is a quickly evolving field of study.

62. Dreaming

Dreams have amused and baffled humanity since the beginning of our species. Originally, people believed dreams to be of spiritual origins. Many saw them as trips into the spirit realm or a chance for spirits to communicate with us. Eventually, humans figured out that there must be a scientific reason why we dream, yet scientists didn't have any theories until recently. Dreams are believed to be our brains' way of processing information from our daily lives. While we sleep, our brain processes memories and thoughts from our waking lives, causing us to recall them through dreams. Some dreams may directly correlate to recent events, others may be more loosely related. In addition, dreams sometimes serve as a means for us to practice certain interactions we may fear or engage in regularly. It's a way that we can rehearse these actions without having to actually do them while awake. Ultimately, dreams exist to benefit us in our waking lives.

63. Getting sunburns

Sunburns are an unpleasant part of summertime. With hot, red skin and a painful itch that can't be scratched, nobody enjoys getting a sunburn. People get sunburned due to exposure to something called ultraviolet light, which is produced by the sun. This light is good for us in small amounts, but too much of it causes the body to react poorly. The immune system is activated whenever the body is exposed to excessive sunlight. This is because this type of light damages our DNA, potentially leading to issues like cancer if left unchecked. The result is the red skin, itchiness, and blisters that we all dislike. It's how our body eliminates damaged cells. This process is exacerbated by increased blood flow to the affected area as part of the healing process, which in turn leads to additional inflammation. Most sunburns heal in a few days, peeling away to reveal fresh skin.

64. Getting bruises

Most people have bumped into corners or have fallen down only to have woken up to a large, painful bruise on their body the next day. Bruises are the result of injuries to the skin and the tissue directly underneath it. When we bump ourselves or are hit by something hard, small capillaries in our skin burst open from the pressure of the hit. This leads to blood spilling out underneath our skin. With nowhere to go, this blood pools underneath our skin causing big, red bruises to form. Soon, the blood begins to lose oxygen and begins to turn either purple or blue. Over time, our body breaks down this blood that remains beneath our skin. More specifically, the body breaks down the hemoglobin in the blood and converts it into yellow-green substances called bilirubin and biliverdin, resulting in a yellowing of the bruise. Ultimately, the bruise will turn brown and then gradually fade away as the body continues to break down and absorb the blood.

65. Liking cute animals

Almost all humans tend to find certain kinds of animals cute. Most individuals find puppies and kittens to be adorable, as well as several other older animals. Why do humans find these animals cute and why do we like cute animals so much? Scientists believe it's because animals evolved to be cute. Humans were more likely to kill creatures who looked gross or ugly. They were also more likely to help the animals that seemed cute if they found them to be in danger. Scientists believe the reason we like cute animals so much is because they remind us of human infants. Often, the features that cute animals have align with features found in human babies, such as having large eyes on a small head. Another reason we may find an animal to be cute is because of the type of interactions we have with it. Even if an animal is not physically cute, we may still find their actions cute if they show intelligence. This is because humans are social creatures who tend to bond with others displaying similar behaviors. Overall, this has led to us preferring animals that match us in looks or behavior.

66. Getting acne

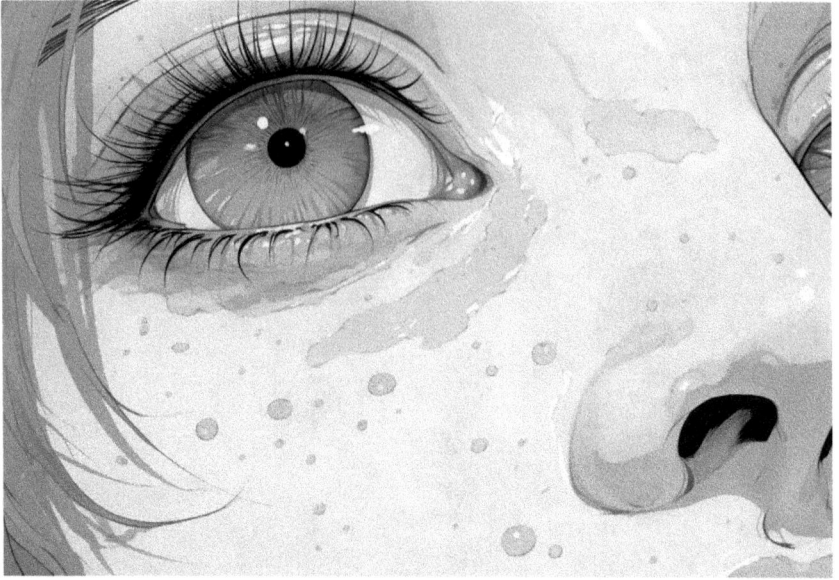

Nobody likes unsightly bumps and pustules on their face. Unfortunately for us, it is a normal part of being a human. Acne is caused when our natural oils, called sebum, clog our pores and hair follicles. Normally, sebum helps keep our skin hydrated and moist. When we make too much sebum or when it's left to collect, it can begin clogging our pores, resulting in acne. If a pore is only partially clogged, it will often turn into a black-headed pimple, which is a mix of dirt and sebum. If it's fully clogged, the pimple produced will have a white head as no dirt is able to enter the pore. Acne is most common during puberty when excess hormones can cause the skin to become more oily than usual, but it usually lessens by adulthood. However, it rarely fully goes away. Most adults will continue getting occasional pimples throughout their lives. Sometimes, acne can be caused by more serious conditions. Skin infections can manifest as acne in certain circumstances and acne can easily worsen when it becomes infected.

67. Getting moles

Moles are growths that appear as black, brown, or tan bumps on the skin. Most are harmless and are simply caused by an excessive amount of melanin-producing cells known as melanocytes, growing in one particular area of the skin. This results in an excessive amount of melanin being produced. Melanin is what gives our skin color; the more melanin produced, the darker our skin is. Sometimes, moles can be cancerous. This is known as melanoma and it's most common in those who are exposed to the sun for long periods of time without sunscreen. If a mole is larger than a pencil eraser, unevenly shaped, contains multiple colors, or changes shape over time, it's important to get it looked at by a doctor. These are sometimes symptoms of melanoma as normal moles are generally small, round, and only one color. However, sometimes even normal moles will have odd traits, making it important to let a doctor be the one to determine whether a mole is safe or not.

68. Getting red eyes when rubbing them

It is extremely uncomfortable when our eyes begin to itch or sting. Thus, it's very common for people to rub their eyes and suddenly find them turning bright red. This can be startling for some, especially if it is the first time they notice it. Why does this happen? The eyes are filled with tiny blood vessels, and these blood vessels are fragile. When one rubs their eyes, these blood vessels break open, causing the eyes to turn red. The blood will disperse after resting your eyes for a short period. However, it is generally not good to rub your eyes if you can avoid it, as it will only increase irritation and can potentially make them itch more. Try using allergy-reducing eye drops or resting them instead when they begin to itch. This can help prevent bloodshot eyes and the beginning of a cycle of itching and rubbing.

69. Stinking when sweating

Many people smell individuals who are sweaty and assume that sweat itself is responsible for the stench. This is actually only partially true. Sweat, on its own, doesn't have a strong odor; it primarily consists of water, salt and occasionally small amounts of fat, none of which produce a foul smell. The smell does not begin until the sweat meets our skin. Humans are home to a multitude of bacteria. When our sweat comes in contact with our skin, it is coming in contact with many different forms of bacteria. This bacteria uses the sweat as a food source, feeding off the salt and fat. This causes the smell we associate with sweat. Different forms of bacteria produce different odors, some of which smell worse than others. Thus, people smell differently when they sweat depending on the specific kind of bacteria they have on their skin. This is why some people smell worse when they sweat than others.

70. Going to the bathroom

Everyone has felt the familiar ache of a full bladder or the painful cramps of an oncoming bowel movement. When we eat and drink, some unnecessary substances are absorbed into our bloodstream. Our kidneys remove these substances from our blood and turn them into urine, which is then stored in our bladders. Once enough urine is present, we get the urge to urinate (or go pee). This releases the waste. Meanwhile, we have bowel movements (or go poo) because of the physical remains of food needing to leave our bodies. Once we have extracted all the nutrients from what we eat, it is sent out of our body via the colon in order to make room for more food. Both of these processes keep us safe and healthy.

71. Crying when sad

Crying is a common reaction to negative emotions such as sadness. Often, it's not controllable and is our natural reaction to difficult situations. Behaviorists believe we developed this reflex due to our social nature. Babies are born unable to speak; they cry as a way to show that they need assistance from caregivers. Behaviorists believe that we never grow out of this reflex; evidence for this theory is found in the components of tears. Tears produced when sad contain more protein, causing them to stick to our faces and be more visible to others. It's essentially a signal that something is wrong and that we need help. In addition, for unknown reasons, crying releases endorphins which are chemicals that make us feel good. This leads to us feeling less stressed and less sad. This results in us feeling less stressed and less sad, which can help us cope if no one comes to our assistance. This is why people often feel better and less sad once they finish crying.

72. Laughing

For a very long time, scientists were unable to determine why humans laugh when they find something funny. Recently, experts have come up with a theory as to why we developed this behavior. People often laugh when something is unexpected and amusing. Scientists believe that this reaction may have originated as a way to show that something originally believed to be dangerous was not actually a threat. For example, a tribe might have been hunting and believed that they were being stalked by a large lion. They may have sent one member of the tribe to go back and try to see the animal that was stalking them. If the member of the tribe going to check instead found that they were being followed by a flamingo, they might laugh at the unexpected situation. This laughter would indicate to the group that there was no threat. This, however, is still just a theory. Scientists are still studying the behavior to this day.

73. Having tonsils

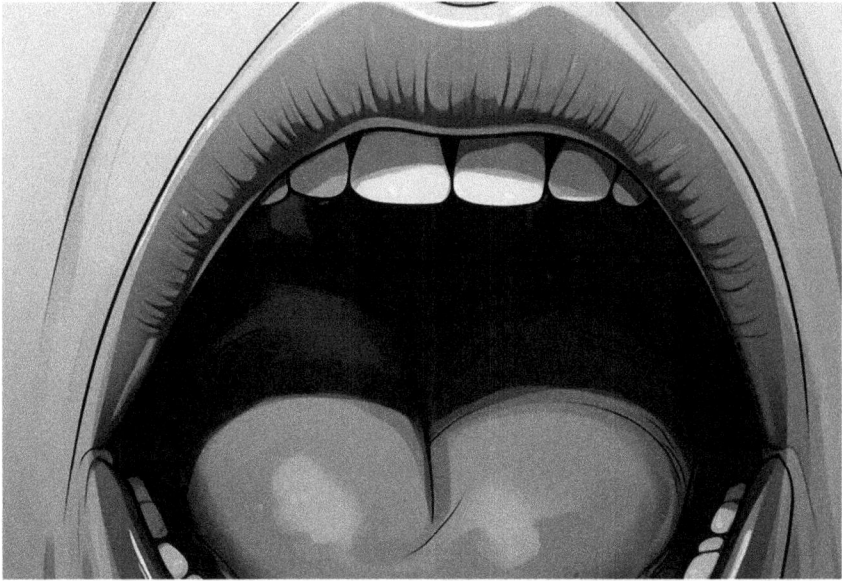

The only time most people hear about tonsils is when they are infected or need to be taken out. Tonsillectomies (removal of the tonsils) are very common surgeries, leading many to wonder what the tonsils are supposed to do for the body. The tonsils sit in the back of the upper throat and are usually visible when one opens their mouth and sticks their tongue out. When they are infected, they may grow larger and grow patches of pus. Tonsils are part of the immune system. They are similar to lymph nodes and they filter out germs that enter your throat in order to prevent illness from getting deeper into the body. They are home to a large number of white blood cells, which activate when germs are nearby in order to destroy them. While this does help fight infection, it's not a necessary body part. Excessive tonsil infections can cause one to feel sick regularly. Doctors may recommend that the tonsils be removed to help prevent these infections. Once the tonsils are removed, the body compensates for the loss in other ways. Most people find themselves healthier after the infected tonsils are removed.

74. Have an appendix

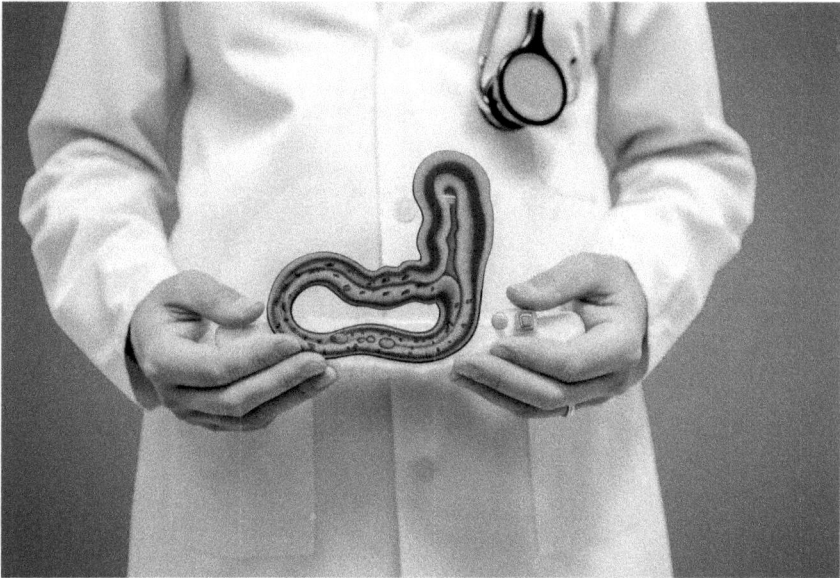

The appendix is an organ that is only spoken about when it is being removed. Appendicitis is a painful condition caused by an infection in this organ. Until recently, many doctors were unaware of why we have this organ to begin with as its purpose is not obvious. The appendix actually has multiple functions, although scientists don't fully understand all of them. It is believed that it holds onto extra healthy bacteria. When the stomach is low on this healthy bacteria, the appendix can release some to return balance to the digestive system. In addition, it seems to play a role in the immune system; specifically, it is linked to immune responses created by the following types of cells: T-lymphocytes and B-lymphocytes. Ultimately, its role in these reactions is not fully understood; however, it has been determined that while the organ is useful, the body is able to function without it if necessary. Thus, in some cases, when the appendix is infected, it is best to remove it.

75. Needing vitamins

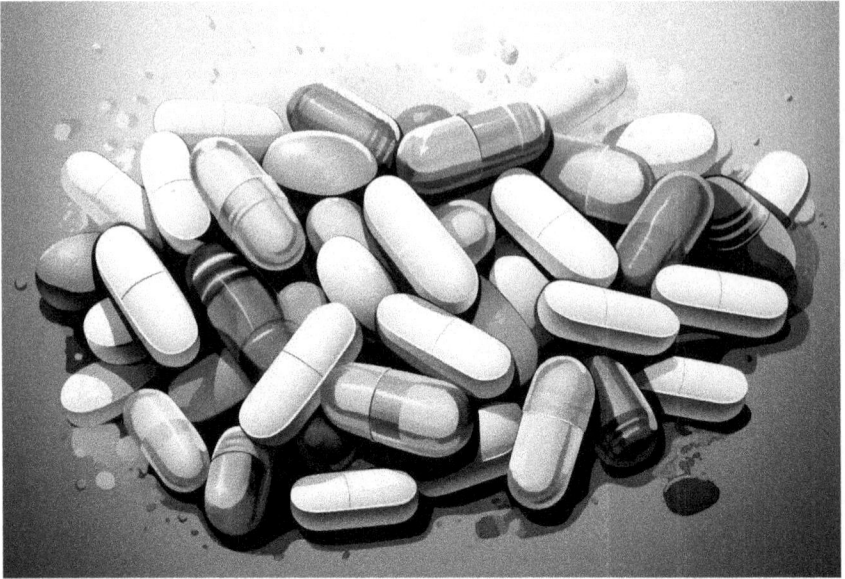

Humans normally get vitamins from the food they eat; sometimes, they get them via supplements; however, not everyone knows the function of them. Vitamins are compounds that help keep various body parts functioning properly. Different vitamins have different uses in the body. Vitamin A primarily helps keep teeth, skin, and bones healthy. Vitamin B helps keep the brain functioning, helps maintain a good metabolism, and increases energy production. Vitamin C helps wounds heal, promotes healthy teeth, and helps boost the immune system. Vitamin D helps the body absorb calcium, which is why it is often added to milk. Calcium helps strengthen bones. Vitamin E helps the body create red blood cells. Vitamin K helps blood clot. These are not the only functions of these vitamins, but they are the most well-known. Vitamins often impact numerous organs and have a variety of uses in the body. By maintaining a healthy diet and getting a proper amount of sunlight, you can ensure you have all the vitamins needed to stay healthy.

76. Drinking coffee

Coffee is a common beverage across the world. It is created from coffee beans, which are dried and ground up. The beans are placed in a filter and hot water is run through them; this bean-infused water is called coffee, and it is often sweetened with sugar or sugar substitutes. Sometimes cream or milk is added to take away some of the bitterness. One common reason people drink coffee is because they enjoy the flavor. Some like the bitter flavor of unsweetened coffee; others like the sweet, creamy flavor of cappuccinos. This, however, is not the only reason to drink coffee. Coffee contains caffeine, which is a stimulant that gives people energy and helps them feel mentally alert. Many people drink coffee for this effect. Coffee also has health benefits; it can boost metabolism and studies have shown that it can improve liver function. Thus, people drink coffee for a variety of reasons.

77. Napping

Napping is something that most humans partake in when young. Some people continue this activity once older, while others stop napping after childhood. As babies, naps are necessary for us to function properly since babies need significantly more sleep than older children and adults. Once humans are past the infant stage, naps are usually taken to help individuals feel more rested later in the day. Children may be encouraged to nap when young as they tend to become cranky when they are tired. Teenagers and adults may nap if they become tired after school or work so that they can wake up feeling refreshed later in the afternoon. This refreshed feeling helps people concentrate and feel better than if they simply fought to stay awake when tired. Sometimes, people will nap due to medical conditions, such as needing to save energy to fight the flu or having a condition such as narcolepsy which forces one to need more sleep. Some people may also nap more when depressed. Overall, naps are usually just a way to regain energy, but they can sometimes be a symptom of a bigger issue.

78. Playing sports

People love playing and watching a variety of sports for a few different reasons. First, they enjoy sports simply because they are fun. Scoring and winning a game can be rewarding, and the physical activity involved can be entertaining. Second, sports are a great way to get exercise. It can be difficult and tedious to exercise, but playing a game can help make the experience more enjoyable. It gives people goals to aim for and adds complexity to the act, keeping everyone engaged. Another reason people play sports is because it helps strengthen bonds with others. Working together on a team can help make friendships stronger. Playing against somebody, but acting in a fair and appropriate manner can also have this effect. Overall, sports are primarily played for entertainment, but they are also sometimes enjoyed for exercise and bonding.

79. Having pets

Humans keep pets for companionship and entertainment purposes; however, this was not always the case. Initially, individuals did not keep pets at all; animals actually played a larger role in the creation of pets than humans did. Wolves began lingering around early humans due to the humans having more meat than they could eat themselves. People often shared this meat with the hungry wolves, which led to them becoming pets. Over time, they lost their wild traits and became dogs. Cats share a similar story, as they began hanging around humans in order to eat the mice that commonly plagued villages. Over time, humans began to use dogs for a variety of tasks and purposely bred cats for pest control. Eventually, working pets became less common and the idea of them as companions took over. This led to other docile animals, such as geckos and hermit crabs, being sold as pets.

80. Enjoying music

Many people have found themselves bouncing along to a song or dancing to their favorite tune and wondering "why does this feel so good?" Humans have enjoyed music since the dawn of time when we only had drums and our voices to make it. This is because of music's effect on the human brain. The human brain's limbic system reacts very strongly to music. This system is responsible for us feeling rewarded after we complete a task. When we listen to music, it activates and releases dopamine; which causes pleasure. In addition, we may enjoy music beyond this basic response. Music can also invoke an emotional response in us, allowing us to feel drawn to music that speaks to us. Sad music may make sad people feel better or less alone; happy music can help individuals celebrate their own happiness. This relational aspect of music also plays a large role in why we enjoy it. Thus, while music naturally causes us to produce dopamine, it also moves us by being relatable.

Did You Know?

- The human nose can detect over one trillion different scents.
- Humans have the capacity to remember up to 100,000 different faces.
- Our eyes are the same size from birth, but our nose and ears continue to grow throughout our lives.
- Humans can hear sounds as low as 20 Hz and as high as 20,000 Hz.
- The human stomach produces a new layer of mucus every two weeks to avoid digesting itself.
- Your brain uses about 20% of the body's oxygen and energy.
- Your hair is strongest when it's wet and more elastic when it's dry.

81. Having panic attacks

Panic attacks are highly unpleasant events that cause humans to feel very anxious and afraid. These attacks can last anywhere from a few minutes to a few hours. Symptoms include a variety of unpleasant effects such as shortness of breath, rapid heart rate, and a feeling of impending doom. Despite how terrifying these events are, they happen due to an important system in our body. The nervous system is primed to respond to threats via the fight or flight response. When our body senses danger, it reacts by getting us ready to fight the dangerous creature or run from it. This leads to us taking in more oxygen, gaining a burst of energy, and getting an urge to react. When this threat response system activates when no physical threat exists, it can result in a panic attack. The body is prepared to fight or run but can do neither, resulting in feelings of fear alongside a variety of other unpleasant symptoms. For some, these attacks happen rarely and are easily managed, while for others, they happen often and may require treatment from a mental health professional.

82. Watching the Super Bowl

For football fans, watching the Super Bowl is a yearly event. Everyone gets food, pours beverages, and settles in to watch the big game. What makes this game so special? The Super Bowl is the championship of American football. Teams play all season long hoping to be able to play in the Super Bowl at the end of the season. Football fans watch this game in order to see who is the best team of the season. Another reason somebody may watch the Super Bowl is for the halftime performance. During halftime, popular musical artists are chosen to perform; and many people tune in to watch these performances. Additionally, many viewers eagerly await the special Super Bowl commercials, for which companies fiercely compete to secure airtime. These commercials are known for their exceptional humor and originality, captivating audiences to the point where some folks primarily watch the game for these entertaining advertisements.

83. Going swimming in pools

Swimming is fun and humans have been doing it long before pools were invented. Originally, people swam in natural bodies of water such as lakes, rivers, seas, and oceans. Now people have the option to swim in pools instead. Swimming in a pool has several benefits that swimming in a natural body of water does not. First, it is cleaner; the cleanliness of pools are controlled by filtering the water and adding either chlorine or salt. This kills germs that can make us sick, something that natural bodies of water cannot do. In addition, pools can be built anywhere, making swimming more accessible. One can build a pool on their property so that they can swim whenever they feel like doing so. A city government can build a pool in order to provide recreation to its citizens. These two factors of cleanliness and convenience are the primary reasons for the popularity of swimming pools.

84. Seeing in color

It's known that not all creatures see the same colors. Some creatures, such as dogs, only see a small amount of colors and are generally known to be colorblind to red and green. Other creatures, such as the mantis shrimp, can see so many colors that some of them are not even visible to humans. What makes us able to see the colors we see and unable to see other colors? Our eyes have cells called cones that help us turn reflections of light into color. They are home to a type of cell called photo pigments that aid in distinguishing between different colors. Our eyes take the information gained from the cones, such as the number of cones activated and how strongly they were activated, and use that information to determine which color we see. Animals that have more of these cones can see a larger amount of colors. It's estimated that humans can see ten million different colors!

85. Voice changes during adolescence

The experience of a changing voice during adolescence is a hallmark of growing up, particularly noticeable in boys. This vocal transformation is rooted in the physical growth of the larynx, or voice box, stimulated by hormonal surges associated with puberty. In boys, the larynx grows larger and the vocal cords lengthen and thicken, causing the voice to drop in pitch. Girls also experience voice changes, but these are typically more subtle since their laryngeal growth is less pronounced. The result is a voice that becomes fuller and more resonant, rather than significantly deeper. This developmental milestone can lead to a period of vocal unpredictability, often characterized by cracks and squeaks, as the adolescent learns to navigate the new tonal landscape of their vocal cords. It's a natural part of growth and typically settles down within a few months to a couple of years.

86. Feeling an itch

Feeling an itch is an everyday sensation that most people experience regularly, but it's more than just a trivial tickle. An itch, or "pruritus," to use the medical term, is a complex interaction between skin cells, nerve fibers, and the brain. It starts when our skin encounters an irritant, setting off a cascade of signals to the spinal cord and then to the brain, which interprets the signal as an itch. Common external causes include insect bites, allergens, chemicals in soaps or clothing, or plants like poison ivy. The body's response is to release histamine and other chemicals into the affected area, which stimulate nerve endings and cause the familiar itchy feeling. Internal factors can be as simple as dry skin, which is why we often itch more in the winter when humidity is low. Other internal causes include systemic conditions like liver disease, kidney failure, or thyroid disorders, and reactions to certain medications. Regardless of the cause, scratching is the body's natural defense mechanism to remove the irritant.

87. Using social media

Social media websites, such as Facebook and Instagram, are a common way to spend one's time on the Internet. However, there is a lot of disagreement on whether or not their usage is healthy. Why do individuals use social media sites anyway? Social media began as a way to stay connected with people who lived far away or who you only had a casual friendship with. Facebook was originally a website where college students could connect with one another, while MySpace was a social media platform that encouraged people to show their individuality to their friends and family. As technology progressed, social media became more popular. Some websites, such as Instagram, encourage people to post pictures of their lives. Other websites, such as Reddit, allow users to remain anonymous and speak to one another. Overall, the concept that each site share is to allow people all over the world to connect. While this is now sometimes used in ways that are harmful, people still generally use it with this purpose in mind.

88. Growing body hair

Many animals grow fur to regulate body temperature and provide protection, but humans do not grow fur. Instead, they have a thin layer of hair covering their bodies. Why is this so? Believe it or not, the thin layer of hair we grow does help regulate our body temperature to some degree, although this is not the only reason we grow hair. When we get cold, our hair will stand up and help insulate us a bit more, trapping some heat so that we warm up. Certain patches of hair have additional purposes. The hair on our heads protects us from the sun. Meanwhile, the hair on our armpits and groin helps protect us from chafing, as these areas tend to rub against each other when we move. By catching sweat and providing cushion, they help us avoid painful wounds. Hair can also serve as a barrier, catching unwanted invaders like bugs and dirt when they land on our bodies. This helps prevent them from entering our bodies and potentially causing illness. Overall, body hair plays an important role for humans, even though it's not as prominent today as it once was.

89. Having earwax

Earwax can be gross and annoying to deal with. Many individuals grapple with excessive earwax production, which can lead to sensations of leaking or ear blockage. However, despite the annoyance it may cause, earwax serves an essential purpose. It provides protection to the ear canal, ensuring that invaders cannot get inside and harm us. These invaders can be large, such as bugs. Earwax is sticky and traps insects, preventing them from doing damage to the eardrum. Sometimes, however, the invaders are smaller. Earwax also traps germs that can lead to ear infections. While not always successful, earwax greatly reduces the number of ear infections humans catch. In fact, most adult humans do not catch ear infections; it is mainly an illness found in children. Earwax also plays a crucial role in moisturizing the ear canal, preventing dryness and itchiness. In essence, our ears rely on earwax for their proper functioning.

90. Having eyelashes

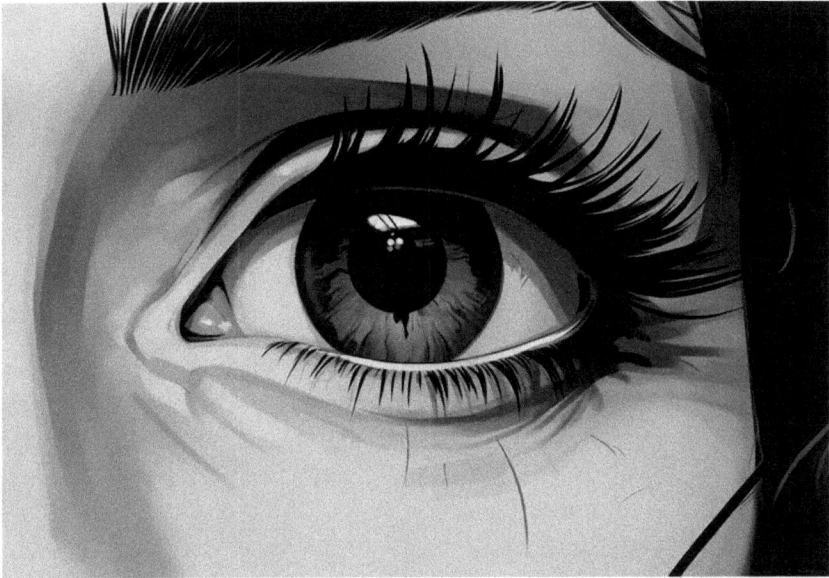

Humans have various types of hair on their bodies, with one type that distinguishes itself from the rest: eyelashes. Eyelashes are thicker than the other hair on the human body, having a consistency similar to cat whiskers, and this serves a specific purpose. Eyelashes help us trap dust and debris so that it does not enter our eyes and do damage. In addition, eyelashes act as sensors for us. If something gets too close to our eyes, the nerves in our eyelash follicles will activate and force us to blink, helping protect our eyes from potential hazards. Eyelashes also play a role in human expression; by fluttering our eyelashes, we can convey flirtatiousness and other emotions. In addition, they are also groomed for specific physical appearances. Many people even wear fake eyelashes so that they look longer. It is essential not to pluck or damage natural eyelashes because they play a crucial role in protecting our eyes.

91. Walking on two legs

Most animals that have four primary limbs do not walk on two legs. Humans and some monkeys seem to be the main exceptions. Why do we walk on two legs, but have four limbs? In addition, why do some of our genetic cousins (monkeys) walk on four legs and some walk on only two? The answer lies in the concept of energy conservation. Humans evolved to be distance hunters. We would follow large animals for miles, stalking them until they lost too much energy to keep up a high speed. Then, we would attack and kill them. This burned a lot of energy. Scientists believe that we evolved to only walk on our legs in order to conserve energy. Studies show that walking on two legs burns 75% less calories than walking on four legs. Saving this energy allowed hunts to last longer when needed and led to less exhaustion afterward. Although we do not engage in distance hunting now, we continue to walk on two legs.

92. Going on maternity leave

The process of pregnancy, childbirth, and caring for an infant is a taxing process on the body and mind. Maternity leave is an extended period of time where pregnant women are allowed to leave their jobs in order to tend to their pregnancies and eventually their babies. Maternity leave sometimes begins before a baby is born. Women with high-risk pregnancies will be allowed to stop work early in order to have bedrest and ensure a safe delivery when the baby comes. For other women, it begins as soon as the baby is born. This allows for the women to recover from childbirth, which can be extremely hard on the body. Women can take up to a few months to return to normal after the event. It also allows women time to bond with their babies, which is crucial during early infancy. Babies develop an attachment to their mothers during this time and having their mother stay home with them aids greatly in this process.

93. Developing crushes

Humans, especially those entering their teenage years, often mention something called "crushes." Crushes are feelings we get when we are attracted to another person. They can evoke excessive happiness, giddiness, self-consciousness, embarrassment, and in some instances, physical discomfort. Why does this happen? Crushes are rooted in our brain's stress and reward system, leading to the release of dopamine, which creates those good feelings, including happiness, reduced tiredness, and decreased hunger. In addition to this, fight or flight-related chemicals are also activated when we are attracted to somebody. Norepinephrine is also released, which makes us feel nervous. Once we begin growing closer to a crush, bonding hormones such as oxytocin are also released, making us feel even stronger towards the person. These processes make it more likely that we will bond with a person and produce children.

94. Making art

Humans love to make art. Even young children can often be found doodling or crafting with glue and paper. Older children may practice drawing and painting. Adults may paint and create models of clay for purposes such as enjoyment or for their careers. Why do we do this? The answer is simple. Art is a form of record-keeping and self-expression. We tell stories via our art, which makes it possible for us to keep records of important feelings and events without having to use words. This is often why ancient people partook in the activity, with cave drawings existing to tell stories of successful hunts and other events. In addition, art helps us express emotions that cannot be expressed in words. By using lines, shading, colors, and a variety of techniques, we can reproduce what we feel on the inside.

95. Hugging

Hugging is a normal part of human life. We hug to show love, comfort others, and as greetings and farewells. Why do we enjoy hugging so much? There are a few reasons why hugs are so pleasurable to humans. The primary reason is that hugs release oxytocin, a hormone that promotes love and bonding. This hormone helps us feel safe and cared about by others, leading to the comforting aspect of hugs and helping us reduce negative feelings such as sadness, anger, and stress. The oxytocin helps override negative emotions and makes us feel safe again. There are also other benefits to hugging. While it is not fully understood, scientists have discovered a link between hugging others and getting sick less often. More hugs apparently correlate to having fewer illnesses throughout one's life. Thus, hugs help us feel good both mentally and physically.

96. Getting ingrown toenails

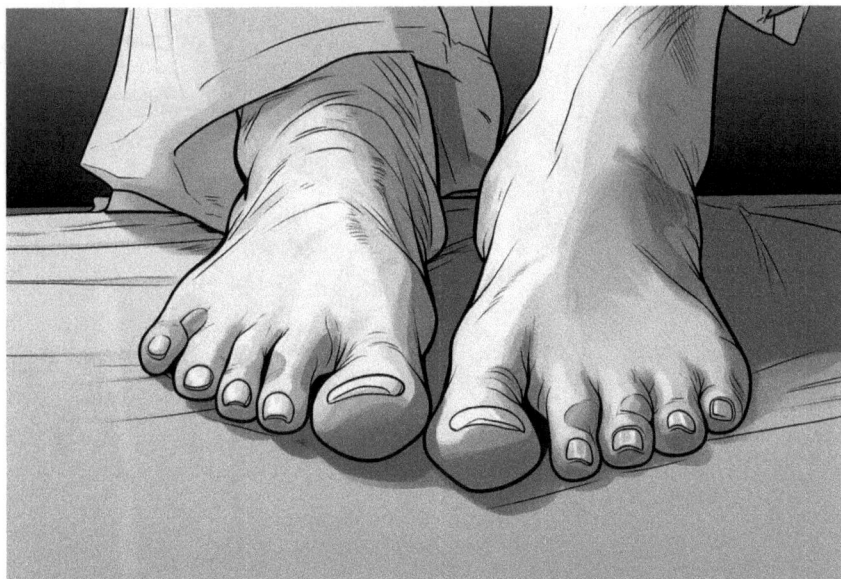

Ingrown toenails are unpleasant. They consist of one corner of a toenail growing into the skin of the toe, piercing delicate tissue and causing pain. If left untreated, ingrown toenails can even become infected. How do they form? Sometimes, ingrown toenails are due to how one is born. Some people simply have toenails that are too big for their toes, causing them to grow into the skin, but this is not often the case. Most cases of ingrown toenails are due to humans doing something they aren't supposed to do, like wearing shoes that are too tight, which can squeeze the toes and cause the nail to enter into the skin. Improper toenail trimming can also cause the nail to grow out at an odd angle, leading to an ingrown toenail. Sometimes, people can fix their ingrown toenails at home by wedging a piece of cotton under the nail so it grows over the toe. Other times, a doctor may have to aid in the removal of the ingrown nail.

97. Shaking hands

Shaking hands is now known as a polite, formal way of greeting somebody you have just met. However, this greeting did not originate as such. The handshake instead began as a firm grasp of the other person's arm. Specifically, when two strangers would meet, they would grasp the other's sword-wielding arm in an attempt to ensure that the other was unable to draw his weapon. Once the other's alliances were determined, the individuals would release each other. This slowly turned into a simple arm clasping to check that the other had no weapon once carrying a sword became less common. This too eventually evolved into reaching out to clasp the forearm as a gesture of greeting unrelated to weaponry. The Quakers, a subset of Christians that promote equality and simplicity, popularized this specific evolution of the action as they felt it was more appropriate than bowing or tipping one's hat. Eventually, the clasp changed to include only the hands. Then, an up-and-down movement was added.

98. Having gardens

Gardening is a hobby that many individuals enjoy. However, it wasn't always a luxury as it tends to be today. Originally, gardens were a necessity. Gardening and farming were essentially the same during the early days of growing food. A tribe or community would grow food and distribute it as needed. Once trade became popular, farming and gardening began to differentiate. Farms were where crops were grown for trade, while gardens were for personal use. Often, peasants working the land during the medieval era would have their own gardens in order to grow their own food alongside the food they were farming. Rich families throughout history often had luxurious gardens full of exotic plants and flowers. Poor families often had well-planned gardens filled with food-bearing plants in order to supplement their diet. Today, people grow gardens as a hobby, to supplement their diets, and to add life to their yards. In some places, community gardens are also returning in order to provide free food to those who may need it.

99. Going on diets

People often hear others state that they need to go on a diet. Some may wonder why people choose to start new diets or certain diets. In general, there are three reasons why one may choose to diet: to lose weight, to get healthier, or to treat an underlying medical condition. Some diets do not necessarily improve the health of the people who follow them but do help individuals lose weight. Calorie-counting alone is a safe diet that falls into this category. In individuals who are overweight, it can lead to health benefits over a period of time. Some diets improve health directly by including key nutrients and excluding unhealthy foods. One example of this is the Mediterranean Diet, which includes healthy fats and a lot of nutrients people tend to lack. Other diets, such as low-salt diets for those with high blood pressure, can be useful when somebody has a medical condition affected by certain foods.

100. Taking probiotics

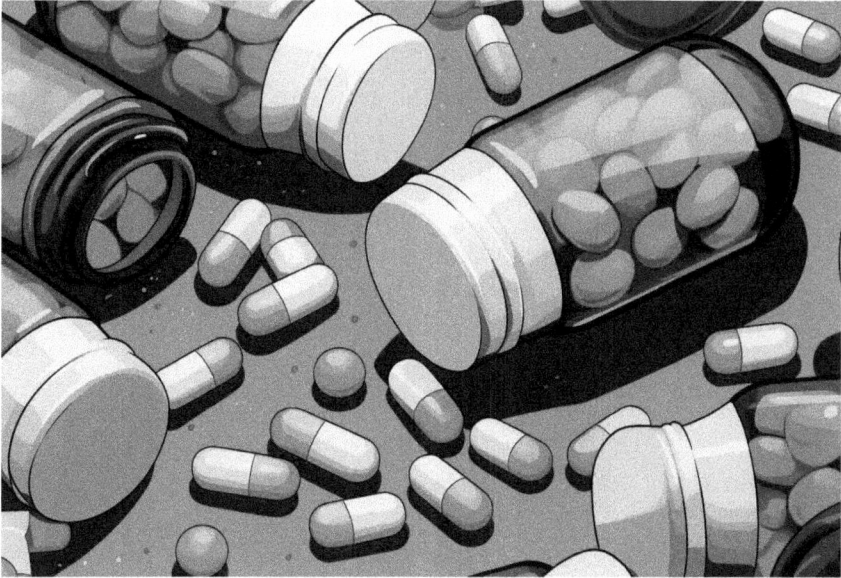

Many people are aware of antibiotics, which is medication given to people to help them fight bacterial infections. However, fewer people have heard of probiotics. While antibiotics get rid of bad bacteria, probiotics do the opposite. Probiotics are pills or supplements that consist of good bacteria. These supplements, when swallowed, release the bacteria into the digestive tract, helping break down food and making digestion easier. Probiotics also help fight off bad bacteria when there is too much of it, as the good bacteria will combat the harmful one. They also aid in preventing bad bacteria from being able to enter the bloodstream by coating the digestive system. Some good bacteria even aid in the production of vitamins as well as help break down and absorb medication. Thus, probiotics are taken in order to create a healthier body and a balance between good and bad bacteria. One of the most common ways people ingest probiotics is by eating yogurt, which naturally contains good bacteria.

Did You Know?

- Humans are the only animals that can intentionally delay sleep.
- The smallest bones in the human body are in the ear, called the ossicles.
- We have a natural aversion to bitter tastes, often associated with potential toxins.
- Humans can differentiate between hot and cold water using only their sense of touch. Our sense of touch is most sensitive on our fingertips and lips.
- Humans are capable of recognizing music across cultures, even if they've never heard that style before.

101. Speaking

Humans are the only animals truly capable of speech. Some animals, such as certain species of birds, can mimic speech to some degree. None are capable of producing their own, however. This is due to the way our bodies are built. When we speak, air from the lungs travels upwards and out. It passes through our trachea and larynx (also known as a voice box or vocal cords). It then is molded by our throat, tongue, teeth, cheeks, and lips in order to produce certain sounds. By changing the size, shape, and position of these body parts, we can produce different sounds. In addition, the stopping and releasing of airflow in certain patterns also aid us in producing different sounds and tones. However, speech starts somewhere else: the brain. There are three areas of the brain associated with speech: Wernicke's area (which creates words), Broca's area (which helps plan sentences), and the motor cortex (which controls muscle movement). Together, the brain tells the body how to move to make sounds.

References

Atkinson, William. How to Read Human Nature: Its Inner States and Outer Forms. DigiCat. 2022.

Campbell, Neil and Kean, Alasdair. American Cultural Studies: An Introduction to American Culture. Taylor & Francis, 2013.

Gislason, Stephen. Human Nature: Innate Properties. Persona Digital. 2017.

Kinsbruner, Jay. Encyclopedia of Latin American History and Culture. Gale, 2008.

Koks, Charlotte. "Culture and Tradition of the USA | Understanding the American Way of Life." Growpro. https://growproexperience.com/en/usa/culture-and-tradition-of-the-usa/. Accessed October 17, 2023.

Langley, Michelle. "Rituals have been crucial for humans throughout history – and we still need them." The Conversation. https://theconversation.com/rituals-have-been-crucial-for-humans-throughout-history-and-we-still-need-them-193951. Accessed September 26, 2023.

McKelvie, Callum and Zimmermann, Kim Ann. "American culture: Traditions and customs of the United States." LiveScience. https://www.livescience.com/28945-american-culture.html. Accessed October 10, 2023.

Morin, Oliver. How Traditions Live and Die. Oxford University Press, 2016.

Penner, Hans. "Ritual." Britannica. https://www.britannica.com/topic/ritual. Accessed October 2, 2023.

Peppas, Lynn. Cultural Traditions in the United Kingdom. Crabtree Publishing Company, 2014.

Rutherford, Adam. The Book of Humans: A Brief History of Culture, Sex, War and the Evolution of Us. Orion, 2018.

Smith, Seldean. "20 Fascinating Cultural Traditions Around the World." DayTranslationsblog. https://www.daytranslations.com/blog/20-traditions-around-the-world/. Accessed October 6, 2023.

Spezio, Michael. "Human Nature, Physical Aspects." http://Encyclopedia.com. https://www.encyclopedia.com/education/encyclopedias-almanacs-transcripts-and-maps/human-nature-physical-aspects/. Accessed October 16, 2023

Bonus!

Thanks for supporting me and purchasing this book! I'd like to send you some freebies. They include:

- The digital version of *500 World War I & II Facts*

- The digital version of *101 Idioms and Phrases*

- The audiobook for my best seller *1144 Random Facts*

Scan the QR code below, enter your email and I'll send you all the files. Happy reading!

Find more of me on Amazon!

Check out the "Amazing Facts" series and learn more about the world around us!

Check out the "Why Do We Say That" series and learn where everyday idioms and phrases come from!

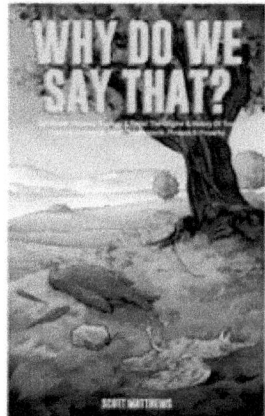

www.ingramcontent.com/pod-product-compliance
Lightning Source LLC
Chambersburg PA
CBHW070124030426
42335CB00016B/2262